O

2022

DAILY PLANNER

PERSONAL INFORMATION

Name:

Address:

City: State: Zip:

Mobile Phone: Home Phone:

Work Phone:

Our Daily Bread
Publishing™

Printed in China

Cover photo: © iStock.com / Derkien

2022

January 2022
S	M	T	W	TH	F	S
						1
2	3	4	5	6	7	8
9	10	11	12	13	14	15
16	17	18	19	20	21	22
23	24	25	26	27	28	29
30	31					

February 2022
S	M	T	W	TH	F	S
		1	2	3	4	5
6	7	8	9	10	11	12
13	14	15	16	17	18	19
20	21	22	23	24	25	26
27	28					

March 2022
S	M	T	W	TH	F	S
		1	2	3	4	5
6	7	8	9	10	11	12
13	14	15	16	17	18	19
20	21	22	23	24	25	26
27	28	29	30	31		

April 2022
S	M	T	W	TH	F	S
					1	2
3	4	5	6	7	8	9
10	11	12	13	14	15	16
17	18	19	20	21	22	23
24	25	26	27	28	29	30

May 2022
S	M	T	W	TH	F	S
1	2	3	4	5	6	7
8	9	10	11	12	13	14
15	16	17	18	19	20	21
22	23	24	25	26	27	28
29	30	31				

June 2022
S	M	T	W	TH	F	S
			1	2	3	4
5	6	7	8	9	10	11
12	13	14	15	16	17	18
19	20	21	22	23	24	25
26	27	28	29	30		

July 2022
S	M	T	W	TH	F	S
					1	2
3	4	5	6	7	8	9
10	11	12	13	14	15	16
17	18	19	20	21	22	23
24	25	26	27	28	29	30
31						

August 2022
S	M	T	W	TH	F	S
	1	2	3	4	5	6
7	8	9	10	11	12	13
14	15	16	17	18	19	20
21	22	23	24	25	26	27
28	29	30	31			

September 2022
S	M	T	W	TH	F	S
				1	2	3
4	5	6	7	8	9	10
11	12	13	14	15	16	17
18	19	20	21	22	23	24
25	26	27	28	29	30	

October 2022
S	M	T	W	TH	F	S
						1
2	3	4	5	6	7	8
9	10	11	12	13	14	15
16	17	18	19	20	21	22
23	24	25	26	27	28	29
30	31					

November 2022
S	M	T	W	TH	F	S
		1	2	3	4	5
6	7	8	9	10	11	12
13	14	15	16	17	18	19
20	21	22	23	24	25	26
27	28	29	30			

December 2022
S	M	T	W	TH	F	S
				1	2	3
4	5	6	7	8	9	10
11	12	13	14	15	16	17
18	19	20	21	22	23	24
25	26	27	28	29	30	31

For the Spirit God gave us does not make us timid, but gives us power, love and self-discipline.

2 TIMOTHY 1:7

2023

January 2023
S	M	T	W	TH	F	S
1	2	3	4	5	6	7
8	9	10	11	12	13	14
15	16	17	18	19	20	21
22	23	24	25	26	27	28
29	30	31				

February 2023
S	M	T	W	TH	F	S
			1	2	3	4
5	6	7	8	9	10	11
12	13	14	15	16	17	18
19	20	21	22	23	24	25
26	27	28				

March 2023
S	M	T	W	TH	F	S
			1	2	3	4
5	6	7	8	9	10	11
12	13	14	15	16	17	18
19	20	21	22	23	24	25
26	27	28	29	30	31	

April 2023
S	M	T	W	TH	F	S
						1
2	3	4	5	6	7	8
9	10	11	12	13	14	15
16	17	18	19	20	21	22
23	24	25	26	27	28	29
30						

May 2023
S	M	T	W	TH	F	S
	1	2	3	4	5	6
7	8	9	10	11	12	13
14	15	16	17	18	19	20
21	22	23	24	25	26	27
28	29	30	31			

June 2023
S	M	T	W	TH	F	S
				1	2	3
4	5	6	7	8	9	10
11	12	13	14	15	16	17
18	19	20	21	22	23	24
25	26	27	28	29	30	

July 2023
S	M	T	W	TH	F	S
						1
2	3	4	5	6	7	8
9	10	11	12	13	14	15
16	17	18	19	20	21	22
23	24	25	26	27	28	29
30	31					

August 2023
S	M	T	W	TH	F	S
		1	2	3	4	5
6	7	8	9	10	11	12
13	14	15	16	17	18	19
20	21	22	23	24	25	26
27	28	29	30	31		

September 2023
S	M	T	W	TH	F	S
					1	2
3	4	5	6	7	8	9
10	11	12	13	14	15	16
17	18	19	20	21	22	23
24	25	26	27	28	29	30

October 2023
S	M	T	W	TH	F	S
1	2	3	4	5	6	7
8	9	10	11	12	13	14
15	16	17	18	19	20	21
22	23	24	25	26	27	28
29	30	31				

November 2023
S	M	T	W	TH	F	S
			1	2	3	4
5	6	7	8	9	10	11
12	13	14	15	16	17	18
19	20	21	22	23	24	25
26	27	28	29	30		

December 2023
S	M	T	W	TH	F	S
					1	2
3	4	5	6	7	8	9
10	11	12	13	14	15	16
17	18	19	20	21	22	23
24	25	26	27	28	29	30
31						

Have I not commanded you? Be strong and courageous. Do not be afraid; do not be discouraged, for the LORD your God will be with you wherever you go.

JOSHUA 1:9

Bible Reading Schedule

JANUARY
1   Gen. 1–3; Mt. 1
2   Gen. 4–6; Mt. 2
3   Gen. 7–9; Mt. 3
4   Gen. 10–12; Mt. 4
5   Gen. 13–15; Mt. 5:1–26
6   Gen. 16–17; Mt. 5:27–48
7   Gen. 18–19; Mt. 6:1–18
8   Gen. 20–22; Mt. 6:19–34
9   Gen. 23–24; Mt. 7
10   Gen. 25–26; Mt. 8:1–17
11   Gen. 27–28; Mt. 8:18–34
12   Gen. 29–30; Mt. 9:1–17
13   Gen. 31–32; Mt. 9:18–38
14   Gen. 33–35; Mt. 10:1–20
15   Gen. 36–38; Mt. 10:21–42
16   Gen. 39–40; Mt. 11
17   Gen. 41–42; Mt. 12:1–23
18   Gen. 43–45; Mt. 12:24–50
19   Gen. 46–48; Mt. 13:1–30
20   Gen. 49–50; Mt. 13:31–58
21   Ex. 1–3; Mt. 14:1–21
22   Ex. 4–6; Mt. 14:22–36
23   Ex. 7–8; Mt. 15:1–20
24   Ex. 9–11; Mt. 15:21–39
25   Ex. 12–13; Mt. 16
26   Ex. 14–15; Mt. 17
27   Ex. 16–18; Mt. 18:1–20
28   Ex. 19–20; Mt. 18:21–35
29   Ex. 21–22; Mt. 19
30   Ex. 23–24; Mt. 20:1–16
31   Ex. 25–26; Mt. 20:17–34

FEBRUARY
1   Ex. 27–28; Mt. 21:1–22
2   Ex. 29–30; Mt. 21:23–46
3   Ex. 31–33; Mt. 22:1–22
4   Ex. 34–35; Mt. 22:23–46
5   Ex. 36–38; Mt. 23:1–22
6   Ex. 39–40; Mt. 23:23–39
7   Lev. 1–3; Mt. 24:1–28
8   Lev. 4–5; Mt. 24:29–51
9   Lev. 6–7; Mt. 25:1–30
10   Lev. 8–10; Mt. 25:31–46
11   Lev. 11–12; Mt. 26:1–25
12   Lev. 13; Mt. 26:26–50
13   Lev. 14; Mt. 26:51–75
14   Lev. 15–16; Mt. 27:1–26

15   Lev. 17–18; Mt. 27:27–50
16   Lev. 19–20; Mt. 27:51–66
17   Lev. 21–22; Mt. 28
18   Lev. 23–24; Mk. 1:1–22
19   Lev. 25; Mk. 1:23–45
20   Lev. 26–27; Mk. 2
21   Num. 1–3; Mk. 3
22   Num. 4–6; Mk. 4:1–20
23   Num. 7–8; Mk. 4:21–41
24   Num. 9–11; Mk. 5:1–20
25   Num. 12–14; Mk. 5:21–43
26   Num. 15–16; Mk. 6:1–29
27   Num. 17–19; Mk. 6:30–56
28   Num. 20–22; Mk. 7:1–13

MARCH
1   Num. 23–25; Mk. 7:14–37
2   Num. 26–27; Mk. 8:1–21
3   Num. 28–30; Mk. 8:22–38
4   Num. 31–33; Mk. 9:1–29
5   Num. 34–36; Mk. 9:30–50
6   Dt. 1–2; Mk. 10:1–31
7   Dt. 3–4; Mk. 10:32–52
8   Dt. 5–7; Mk. 11:1–18
9   Dt. 8–10; Mk. 11:19–33
10   Dt. 11–13; Mk. 12:1–27
11   Dt. 14–16; Mk. 12:28–44
12   Dt. 17–19; Mk. 13:1–20
13   Dt. 20–22; Mk. 13:21–37
14   Dt. 23–25; Mk. 14:1–26
15   Dt. 26–27; Mk. 14:27–53
16   Dt. 28–29; Mk. 14:54–72
17   Dt. 30–31; Mk. 15:1–25
18   Dt. 32–34; Mk. 15:26–47
19   Josh. 1–3; Mk. 16
20   Josh. 4–6; Lk. 1:1–20
21   Josh. 7–9; Lk. 1:21–38
22   Josh. 10–12; Lk. 1:39–56
23   Josh. 13–15; Lk. 1:57–80
24   Josh. 16–18; Lk. 2:1–24
25   Josh. 19–21; Lk. 2:25–52
26   Josh. 22–24; Lk. 3
27   Jud. 1–3; Lk. 4:1–30
28   Jud. 4–6; Lk. 4:31–44
29   Jud. 7–8; Lk. 5:1–16
30   Jud. 9–10; Lk. 5:17–39
31   Jud. 11–12; Lk. 6:1–26

Bible Reading Schedule

APRIL
1   Jud. 13–15; Lk. 6:27–49
2   Jud. 16–18; Lk. 7:1–30
3   Jud. 19–21; Lk. 7:31–50
4   Ruth 1–4; Lk. 8:1–25
5   1 Sam. 1–3; Lk. 8:26–56
6   1 Sam. 4–6; Lk. 9:1–17
7   1 Sam. 7–9; Lk. 9:18–36
8   1 Sam. 10–12; Lk. 9:37–62
9   1 Sam. 13–14; Lk. 10:1–24
10   1 Sam. 15–16; Lk. 10:25–42
11   1 Sam. 17–18; Lk. 11:1–28
12   1 Sam. 19–21; Lk. 11:29–54
13   1 Sam. 22–24; Lk. 12:1–31
14   1 Sam. 25–26; Lk. 12:32–59
15   1 Sam. 27–29; Lk. 13:1–22
16   1 Sam. 30–31; Lk. 13:23–35
17   2 Sam. 1–2; Lk. 14:1–24
18   2 Sam. 3–5; Lk. 14:25–35
19   2 Sam. 6–8; Lk. 15:1–10
20   2 Sam. 9–11; Lk. 15:11–32
21   2 Sam. 12–13; Lk. 16
22   2 Sam. 14–15; Lk. 17:1–19
23   2 Sam. 16–18; Lk. 17:20–37
24   2 Sam. 19–20; Lk. 18:1–23
25   2 Sam. 21–22; Lk. 18:24–43
26   2 Sam. 23–24; Lk. 19:1–27
27   1 Ki. 1–2; Lk. 19:28–48
28   1 Ki. 3–5; Lk. 20:1–26
29   1 Ki. 6–7; Lk. 20:27–47
30   1 Ki. 8–9; Lk. 21:1–19

MAY
1   1 Ki. 10–11; Lk. 21:20–38
2   1 Ki. 12–13; Lk. 22:1–20
3   1 Ki. 14–15; Lk. 22:21–46
4   1 Ki. 16–18; Lk. 22:47–71
5   1 Ki. 19–20; Lk. 23:1–25
6   1 Ki. 21–22; Lk. 23:26–56
7   2 Ki. 1–3; Lk. 24:1–35
8   2 Ki. 4–6; Lk. 24:36–53
9   2 Ki. 7–9; Jn. 1:1–28
10   2 Ki. 10–12; Jn. 1:29–51
11   2 Ki. 13–14; Jn. 2
12   2 Ki. 15–16; Jn. 3:1–18
13   2 Ki. 17–18; Jn. 3:19–36
14   2 Ki. 19–21; Jn. 4:1–30
15   2 Ki. 22–23; Jn. 4:31–54
16   2 Ki. 24–25; Jn. 5:1–24
17   1 Chr. 1–3; Jn. 5:25–47
18   1 Chr. 4–6; Jn. 6:1–21
19   1 Chr. 7–9; Jn. 6:22–44
20   1 Chr. 10–12; Jn. 6:45–71
21   1 Chr. 13–15; Jn. 7:1–27
22   1 Chr. 16–18; Jn. 7:28–53
23   1 Chr. 19–21; Jn. 8:1–27
24   1 Chr. 22–24; Jn. 8:28–59
25   1 Chr. 25–27; Jn. 9:1–23
26   1 Chr. 28–29; Jn. 9:24–41
27   2 Chr. 1–3; Jn. 10:1–23
28   2 Chr. 4–6; Jn. 10:24–42
29   2 Chr. 7–9; Jn. 11:1–29
30   2 Chr. 10–12; Jn. 11:30–57
31   2 Chr. 13–14; Jn. 12:1–26

JUNE
1   2 Chr. 15–16; Jn. 12:27–50
2   2 Chr. 17–18; Jn. 13:1–20
3   2 Chr. 19–20; Jn. 13:21–38
4   2 Chr. 21–22; Jn. 14
5   2 Chr. 23–24; Jn. 15
6   2 Chr. 25–27; Jn. 16
7   2 Chr. 28–29; Jn. 17
8   2 Chr. 30–31; Jn. 18:1–18
9   2 Chr. 32–33; Jn. 18:19–40
10   2 Chr. 34–36; Jn. 19:1–22
11   Ezra 1–2; Jn. 19:23–42
12   Ezra 3–5; Jn. 20
13   Ezra 6–8; Jn. 21
14   Ezra 9–10; Acts 1
15   Neh. 1–3; Acts 2:1–21
16   Neh. 4–6; Acts 2:22–47
17   Neh. 7–9; Acts 3
18   Neh. 10–11; Acts 4:1–22
19   Neh. 12–13; Acts 4:23–37
20   Est. 1–2; Acts 5:1–21
21   Est. 3–5; Acts 5:22–42
22   Est. 6–8; Acts 6
23   Est. 9–10; Acts 7:1–21
24   Job 1–2; Acts 7:22–43
25   Job 3–4; Acts 7:44–60
26   Job 5–7; Acts 8:1–25
27   Job 8–10; Acts 8:26–40
28   Job 11–13; Acts 9:1–21
29   Job 14–16; Acts 9:22–43
30   Job 17–19; Acts 10:1–23

Bible Reading Schedule

JULY

- 1 Job 20–21; Acts 10:24–48
- 2 Job 22–24; Acts 11
- 3 Job 25–27; Acts 12
- 4 Job 28–29; Acts 13:1–25
- 5 Job 30–31; Acts 13:26–52
- 6 Job 32–33; Acts 14
- 7 Job 34–35; Acts 15:1–21
- 8 Job 36–37; Acts 15:22–41
- 9 Job 38–40; Acts 16:1–21
- 10 Job 41–42; Acts 16:22–40
- 11 Ps. 1–3; Acts 17:1–15
- 12 Ps. 4–6; Acts 17:16–34
- 13 Ps. 7–9; Acts 18
- 14 Ps. 10–12; Acts 19:1–20
- 15 Ps. 13–15; Acts 19:21–41
- 16 Ps. 16–17; Acts 20:1–16
- 17 Ps. 18–19; Acts 20:17–38
- 18 Ps. 20–22; Acts 21:1–17
- 19 Ps. 23–25; Acts 21:18–40
- 20 Ps. 26–28; Acts 22
- 21 Ps. 29–30; Acts 23:1–15
- 22 Ps. 31–32; Acts 23:16–35
- 23 Ps. 33–34; Acts 24
- 24 Ps. 35–36; Acts 25
- 25 Ps. 37–39; Acts 26
- 26 Ps. 40–42; Acts 27:1–26
- 27 Ps. 43–45; Acts 27:27–44
- 28 Ps. 46–48; Acts 28
- 29 Ps. 49–50; Rom. 1
- 30 Ps. 51–53; Rom. 2
- 31 Ps. 54–56; Rom. 3

AUGUST

- 1 Ps. 57–59; Rom. 4
- 2 Ps. 60–62; Rom. 5
- 3 Ps. 63–65; Rom. 6
- 4 Ps. 66–67; Rom. 7
- 5 Ps. 68–69; Rom. 8:1–21
- 6 Ps. 70–71; Rom. 8:22–39
- 7 Ps. 72–73; Rom. 9:1–15
- 8 Ps. 74–76; Rom. 9:16–33
- 9 Ps. 77–78; Rom. 10
- 10 Ps. 79–80; Rom. 11:1–18
- 11 Ps. 81–83; Rom. 11:19–36
- 12 Ps. 84–86; Rom. 12
- 13 Ps. 87–88; Rom. 13
- 14 Ps. 89–90; Rom. 14
- 15 Ps. 91–93; Rom. 15:1–13
- 16 Ps. 94–96; Rom. 15:14–33
- 17 Ps. 97–99; Rom. 16
- 18 Ps. 100–102; 1 Cor. 1
- 19 Ps. 103–104; 1 Cor. 2
- 20 Ps. 105–106; 1 Cor. 3
- 21 Ps. 107–109; 1 Cor. 4
- 22 Ps. 110–112; 1 Cor. 5
- 23 Ps. 113–115; 1 Cor. 6
- 24 Ps. 116–118; 1 Cor. 7:1–19
- 25 Ps. 119:1–88; 1 Cor. 7:20–40
- 26 Ps. 119:89–176; 1 Cor. 8
- 27 Ps. 120–122; 1 Cor. 9
- 28 Ps. 123–125; 1 Cor. 10:1–18
- 29 Ps. 126–128; 1 Cor. 10:19–33
- 30 Ps. 129–131; 1 Cor. 11:1–16
- 31 Ps. 132–134; 1 Cor. 11:17–34

SEPTEMBER

- 1 Ps. 135–136; 1 Cor. 12
- 2 Ps. 137–139; 1 Cor. 13
- 3 Ps. 140–142; 1 Cor. 14:1–20
- 4 Ps. 143–145; 1 Cor. 14:21–40
- 5 Ps. 146–147; 1 Cor. 15:1–28
- 6 Ps. 148–150; 1 Cor. 15:29–58
- 7 Prov. 1–2; 1 Cor. 16
- 8 Prov. 3–5; 2 Cor. 1
- 9 Prov. 6–7; 2 Cor. 2
- 10 Prov. 8–9; 2 Cor. 3
- 11 Prov. 10–12; 2 Cor. 4
- 12 Prov. 13–15; 2 Cor. 5
- 13 Prov. 16–18; 2 Cor. 6
- 14 Prov. 19–21; 2 Cor. 7
- 15 Prov. 22–24; 2 Cor. 8
- 16 Prov. 25–26; 2 Cor. 9
- 17 Prov. 27–29; 2 Cor. 10
- 18 Prov. 30–31; 2 Cor. 11:1–15
- 19 Eccl. 1–3; 2 Cor. 11:16–33
- 20 Eccl. 4–6; 2 Cor. 12
- 21 Eccl. 7–9; 2 Cor. 13
- 22 Eccl. 10–12; Gal. 1
- 23 Song 1–3; Gal. 2
- 24 Song 4–5; Gal. 3
- 25 Song 6–8; Gal. 4
- 26 Isa. 1–2; Gal. 5
- 27 Isa. 3–4; Gal. 6
- 28 Isa. 5–6; Eph. 1
- 29 Isa. 7–8; Eph. 2
- 30 Isa. 9–10; Eph. 3

Bible Reading Schedule

OCTOBER

- 1 Isa. 11–13; Eph. 4
- 2 Isa. 14–16; Eph. 5:1–16
- 3 Isa. 17–19; Eph. 5:17–33
- 4 Isa. 20–22; Eph. 6
- 5 Isa. 23–25; Phil. 1
- 6 Isa. 26–27; Phil. 2
- 7 Isa. 28–29; Phil. 3
- 8 Isa. 30–31; Phil 4
- 9 Isa. 32–33; Col. 1
- 10 Isa. 34–36; Col. 2
- 11 Isa. 37–38; Col. 3
- 12 Isa. 39–40; Col. 4
- 13 Isa. 41–42; 1 Th. 1
- 14 Isa. 43–44; 1 Th. 2
- 15 Isa. 45–46; 1 Th. 3
- 16 Isa. 47–49; 1 Th. 4
- 17 Isa. 50–52; 1 Th. 5
- 18 Isa. 53–55; 2 Th. 1
- 19 Isa. 56–58; 2 Th. 2
- 20 Isa. 59–61; 2 Th. 3
- 21 Isa. 62–64; 1 Tim. 1
- 22 Isa. 65–66; 1 Tim. 2
- 23 Jer. 1–2; 1 Tim. 3
- 24 Jer. 3–5; 1 Tim. 4
- 25 Jer. 6–8; 1 Tim. 5
- 26 Jer. 9–11; 1 Tim. 6
- 27 Jer. 12–14; 2 Tim. 1
- 28 Jer. 15–17; 2 Tim. 2
- 29 Jer. 18–19; 2 Tim. 3
- 30 Jer. 20–21; 2 Tim. 4
- 31 Jer. 22–23; Ti. 1

NOVEMBER

- 1 Jer. 24–26; Ti. 2
- 2 Jer. 27–29; Ti. 3
- 3 Jer. 30–31; Philemon
- 4 Jer. 32–33; Heb. 1
- 5 Jer. 34–36; Heb. 2
- 6 Jer. 37–39; Heb. 3
- 7 Jer. 40–42; Heb. 4
- 8 Jer. 43–45; Heb. 5
- 9 Jer. 46–47; Heb. 6
- 10 Jer. 48–49; Heb. 7
- 11 Jer. 50; Heb. 8
- 12 Jer. 51–52; Heb. 9
- 13 Lam. 1–2; Heb. 10:1–18
- 14 Lam. 3–5; Heb. 10:19–39
- 15 Ezek. 1–2; Heb. 11:1–19
- 16 Ezek. 3–4; Heb. 11:20–40
- 17 Ezek. 5–7; Heb. 12
- 18 Ezek. 8–10; Heb. 13
- 19 Ezek. 11–13; Jas. 1
- 20 Ezek. 14–15; Jas. 2
- 21 Ezek. 16–17; Jas. 3
- 22 Ezek. 18–19; Jas. 4
- 23 Ezek. 20–21; Jas. 5
- 24 Ezek. 22–23; 1 Pet. 1
- 25 Ezek. 24–26; 1 Pet. 2
- 26 Ezek. 27–29; 1 Pet. 3
- 27 Ezek. 30–32; 1 Pet. 4
- 28 Ezek. 33–34; 1 Pet. 5
- 29 Ezek. 35–36; 2 Pet. 1
- 30 Ezek. 37–39; 2 Pet. 2

DECEMBER

- 1 Ezek. 40–41; 2 Pet. 3
- 2 Ezek. 42–44; 1 Jn. 1
- 3 Ezek. 45–46; 1 Jn. 2
- 4 Ezek. 47–48; 1 Jn. 3
- 5 Dan. 1–2; 1 Jn. 4
- 6 Dan. 3–4; 1 Jn. 5
- 7 Dan. 5–7; 2 John
- 8 Dan. 8–10; 3 John
- 9 Dan. 11–12; Jude
- 10 Hos. 1–4; Rev. 1
- 11 Hos. 5–8; Rev. 2
- 12 Hos. 9–11; Rev. 3
- 13 Hos. 12–14; Rev. 4
- 14 Joel 1–3; Rev. 5
- 15 Amos 1–3; Rev. 6
- 16 Amos 4–6; Rev. 7
- 17 Amos 7–9; Rev. 8
- 18 Obadiah; Rev. 9
- 19 Jonah 1–4; Rev. 10
- 20 Mic. 1–3; Rev. 11
- 21 Mic. 4–5; Rev. 12
- 22 Mic. 6–7; Rev. 13
- 23 Nahum 1–3; Rev. 14
- 24 Habakkuk 1–3; Rev. 15
- 25 Zephaniah 1–3; Rev. 16
- 26 Haggai 1–2; Rev. 17
- 27 Zech. 1–4; Rev. 18
- 28 Zech. 5–8; Rev. 19
- 29 Zech. 9–12; Rev. 20
- 30 Zech. 13–14; Rev. 21
- 31 Malachi 1–4; Rev. 22

Shopping List

December 2021

S	M	T	W	TH	F	S
			1	2	3	4
5	6	7	8	9	10	11
12	13	14	15	16	17	18
19	20	21	22	23	24	25
26	27	28	29	30	31	

January 2022

S	M	T	W	TH	F	S
						1
2	3	4	5	6	7	8
9	10	11	12	13	14	15
16	17	18	19	20	21	22
23	24	25	26	27	28	29
30	31					

2021–2022

DEC–JAN

Sunday 26

Monday 27

Tuesday 28

Wednesday 29

Thursday 30

Friday 31 New Year's Eve

Saturday 1 New Year's Day

To-Do List

✓

Uncharted Waters

When you pass through the waters, I will be with you.   ISAIAH 43:2

The ball drops in New York's Times Square. The crowd counts down to Big Ben chiming. Sydney Harbor erupts in fireworks. However your city marks it, there's something exciting about welcoming in a new year and the fresh start it brings. On New Year's Day we push out into new waters. What friendships and opportunities might we find?

For all its excitement, though, a new year can be unsettling. None of us knows the future or what storms it may hold. Many New Year's traditions reflect this: Fireworks were invented in China to supposedly ward off evil spirits and make a new season prosperous. And New Year's resolutions date back to the Babylonians who made vows to appease their gods. Such acts were an attempt to make an unknown future secure.

When they weren't making vows, the Babylonians were busy conquering people—including Israel. In time, God sent the enslaved Jews this message: "Do not fear. . . . When you pass through the waters, I will be with you" (Isaiah 43:1-2). Later, Jesus said something similar when He and the disciples were caught sailing in a violent storm. "Why are you so afraid?" He told them before commanding the waters to be still (Matthew 8:23-27).

Today we push out from the shore into new, uncharted waters. Whatever we face, He's with us—and He has the power to calm the waves.

SHERIDAN VOYSEY

Photo: Samburu National Reserve, Kenya
© Darrell Gulin

JANUARY

Sunday	Monday	Tuesday	Wednesday
2	3	4	5
9	10	11	12
16	17	18	19
23	24 Martin Luther King Jr. Day	25	26
30	31		

Sing to the L{ORD} a new song, for he has done marvelous things; his right hand and his holy arm have worked salvation for him. —PSALM 98:1

Thursday	Friday	Saturday	Notes
		1 New Year's Day	
6 Epiphany	7	8	
13	14	15	
20	21	22	
27	28	29	

January 2022

S	M	T	W	TH	F	S
						1
2	3	4	5	6	7	8
9	10	11	12	13	14	15
16	17	18	19	20	21	22
23	24	25	26	27	28	29
30	31					

February 2022

S	M	T	W	TH	F	S
		1	2	3	4	5
6	7	8	9	10	11	12
13	14	15	16	17	18	19
20	21	22	23	24	25	26
27	28					

Shopping List

✓

2022

JANUARY

Sunday 2

Monday 3

Tuesday 4

Wednesday 5

Thursday 6 Epiphany

Friday 7

Saturday 8

To-Do List

✓

Shopping List

January 2022

S	M	T	W	TH	F	S
						1
2	3	4	5	6	7	8
9	10	11	12	13	14	15
16	17	18	19	20	21	22
23	24	25	26	27	28	29
30	31					

February 2022

S	M	T	W	TH	F	S
		1	2	3	4	5
6	7	8	9	10	11	12
13	14	15	16	17	18	19
20	21	22	23	24	25	26
27	28					

2022

JANUARY

Sunday 9

Monday 10

Tuesday 11

Wednesday 12

Thursday 13

Friday 14

Saturday 15

To-Do List

✓

Shopping List

January 2022

S	M	T	W	TH	F	S
						1
2	3	4	5	6	7	8
9	10	11	12	13	14	15
16	17	18	19	20	21	22
23	24	25	26	27	28	29
30	31					

February 2022

S	M	T	W	TH	F	S
		1	2	3	4	5
6	7	8	9	10	11	12
13	14	15	16	17	18	19
20	21	22	23	24	25	26
27	28					

2022
JANUARY

Sunday 16

Monday 17 Martin Luther King Jr. Day

Tuesday 18

Wednesday 19

Thursday 20

Friday 21

Saturday 22

To-Do List

Shopping List

January 2022						
S	M	T	W	TH	F	S
						1
2	3	4	5	6	7	8
9	10	11	12	13	14	15
16	17	18	19	20	21	22
23	24	25	26	27	28	29
30	31					

February 2022						
S	M	T	W	TH	F	S
		1	2	3	4	5
6	7	8	9	10	11	12
13	14	15	16	17	18	19
20	21	22	23	24	25	26
27	28					

2022

JANUARY

Sunday 23

Monday 24

Tuesday 25

Wednesday 26

Thursday 27

Friday 28

Saturday 29

To-Do List

✓

Our Compassionate God

You stretch out your hand against the anger of my foes.   **PSALM 138:7**

The winter night was cold when someone threw a large stone through a Jewish child's bedroom window. A star of David had been displayed in the window, along with a menorah to celebrate Hanukkah, the Jewish Festival of Lights. In the child's town of Billings, Montana, thousands of people—many of them believers in Jesus—responded to the hateful act with compassion. Choosing to identify with the hurt and fear of their Jewish neighbors, they pasted pictures of menorahs in their own windows.

As believers in Jesus, we too receive great compassion. Our Savior humbled himself to live among us (John 1:14), identifying with us. On our behalf, He, "being in very nature God, . . . made himself nothing by taking the very nature of a servant" (Philippians 2:6–7). Then, feeling as we feel and weeping as we weep, He died on a cross, sacrificing His life to save ours.

Nothing we struggle with is beyond our Savior's concern. If someone "throws rocks" at our lives, He comforts us. If life brings disappointments, He walks with us through despair. "Though the LORD is exalted, he looks kindly on the lowly; though lofty, he sees them from afar" (Psalm 138:6). In our troubles, He preserves us, stretching out His hand against both "the anger of [our] foes" (v. 7) and our own deepest fears. *Thank you, God, for your compassionate love.*   PATRICIA RAYBON

2022
FEBRUARY

Sunday	Monday	Tuesday	Wednesday
		1	2 Groundhog Day
6	7	8	9
13	14 Valentine's Day	15 Flag Day (Canada)	16
20	21 Presidents' Day	22	23
27	28		

Dear friends, let us love one another, for love comes from God. Everyone who loves has been born of God and knows God. —1 JOHN 4:7-8

Thursday	Friday	Saturday	Notes
3	4	5	
10	11	12	
17	18	19	
24	25	26	

Shopping List

February 2022

S	M	T	W	TH	F	S
		1	2	3	4	5
6	7	8	9	10	11	12
13	14	15	16	17	18	19
20	21	22	23	24	25	26
27	28					

March 2022

S	M	T	W	TH	F	S
		1	2	3	4	5
6	7	8	9	10	11	12
13	14	15	16	17	18	19
20	21	22	23	24	25	26
27	28	29	30	31		

2022
JAN-FEB

Sunday 30

Monday 31

Tuesday 1

Wednesday 2   Groundhog Day

Thursday 3

Friday 4

Saturday 5

To-Do List

✓

Shopping List

February 2022

S	M	T	W	TH	F	S
		1	2	3	4	5
6	7	8	9	10	11	12
13	14	15	16	17	18	19
20	21	22	23	24	25	26
27	28					

March 2022

S	M	T	W	TH	F	S
		1	2	3	4	5
6	7	8	9	10	11	12
13	14	15	16	17	18	19
20	21	22	23	24	25	26
27	28	29	30	31		

2022

FEBRUARY

Sunday 6

Monday 7

Tuesday 8

Wednesday 9

Thursday 10

Friday 11

Saturday 12

To-Do List

✓

Shopping List

✓	

February 2022

S	M	T	W	TH	F	S
		1	2	3	4	5
6	7	8	9	10	11	12
13	14	15	16	17	18	19
20	21	22	23	24	25	26
27	28					

March 2022

S	M	T	W	TH	F	S
		1	2	3	4	5
6	7	8	9	10	11	12
13	14	15	16	17	18	19
20	21	22	23	24	25	26
27	28	29	30	31		

2022

FEBRUARY

Sunday 13

Monday 14 Valentine's Day

Tuesday 15 Flag Day (Canada)

Wednesday 16

Thursday 17

Friday 18

Saturday 19

To-Do List

✓

Shopping List

February 2022

S	M	T	W	TH	F	S
		1	2	3	4	5
6	7	8	9	10	11	12
13	14	15	16	17	18	19
20	21	22	23	24	25	26
27	28					

March 2022

S	M	T	W	TH	F	S
		1	2	3	4	5
6	7	8	9	10	11	12
13	14	15	16	17	18	19
20	21	22	23	24	25	26
27	28	29	30	31		

2022

FEBRUARY

Sunday 20

Monday 21 Presidents' Day

Tuesday 22

Wednesday 23

Thursday 24

Friday 25

Saturday 26

To-Do List

✓

Wandering Off

Rejoice with me; I have found my lost sheep.
LUKE 15:6

Living near cattle ranches as he did, humorist Michael Yaconelli noticed how cows were prone to wander while grazing. A cow would keep moving, always looking for the fabled "greener pastures." Near the edge of the property, the cow might discover some cool fresh grass under a shade tree. Just beyond a broken-down part of the fence was a tasty clump of foliage. Then the cow might push far beyond the fence and out to the road. It slowly "nibbled" its way into being lost.

Cows aren't alone in their roaming problem. Sheep also wander, and it's likely that people have the biggest tendency of all to stray.

Perhaps that's one of the reasons God compares us to sheep in the Bible. It can be easy to meander and "nibble our way" through reckless compromises and foolish decisions, never noticing how far away from the truth we've strayed.

Jesus told the Pharisees the story of a lost sheep. The sheep was of such value to the shepherd that he left his other sheep behind while he searched for the wandering one. And when he found the one that had strayed, he celebrated (Luke 15:1–7)!

Such is the happiness of God over those who turn back to Him. Jesus said, "Rejoice with me; I have found my lost sheep" (v. 6). God has sent us a Savior to rescue us and bring us home.

CINDY HESS KASPER

MARCH

Sunday	Monday	Tuesday	Wednesday
		1	2 Ash Wednesday
6	7	8	9
13 Daylight Saving Time Begins	14 Commonwealth Day (Canada)	15	16
20 First Day of Spring	21	22	23
27	28	29	30

Do not fear, for I am with you; do not be dismayed, for I am your God. I will strengthen you and help you; I will uphold you with my righteous right hand. —ISAIAH 41:10

Thursday	Friday	Saturday	Notes
3	4	5	
10	11	12	
17	18	19	
Purim St. Patrick's Day			
24	25	26	
31			

Shopping List

	March 2022						
	S	M	T	W	TH	F	S
			1	2	3	4	5
	6	7	8	9	10	11	12
	13	14	15	16	17	18	19
	20	21	22	23	24	25	26
	27	28	29	30	31		

	April 2022						
	S	M	T	W	TH	F	S
						1	2
	3	4	5	6	7	8	9
	10	11	12	13	14	15	16
	17	18	19	20	21	22	23
	24	25	26	27	28	29	30

2022
FEB-MAR

Sunday 27

Monday 28

Tuesday 1

Wednesday 2 Ash Wednesday

Thursday 3

Friday 4

Saturday 5

To-Do List

✓

March 2022								April 2022						
S	M	T	W	TH	F	S		S	M	T	W	TH	F	S
		1	2	3	4	5							1	2
6	7	8	9	10	11	12		3	4	5	6	7	8	9
13	14	15	16	17	18	19		10	11	12	13	14	15	16
20	21	22	23	24	25	26		17	18	19	20	21	22	23
27	28	29	30	31				24	25	26	27	28	29	30

Shopping List

✓

2022

MARCH

Sunday 6

Monday 7

Tuesday 8

Wednesday 9

Thursday 10

Friday 11

Saturday 12

To-Do List

✓

Shopping List

March 2022						
S	M	T	W	TH	F	S
		1	2	3	4	5
6	7	8	9	10	11	12
13	14	15	16	17	18	19
20	21	22	23	24	25	26
27	28	29	30	31		

April 2022						
S	M	T	W	TH	F	S
					1	2
3	4	5	6	7	8	9
10	11	12	13	14	15	16
17	18	19	20	21	22	23
24	25	26	27	28	29	30

2022
MARCH

Sunday 13 Daylight Saving Time Begins

Monday 14 Commonwealth Day (Canada)

Tuesday 15

Wednesday 16

Thursday 17 Purim
St. Patrick's Day

Friday 18

Saturday 19

To-Do List

✓

Shopping List

March 2022						
S	M	T	W	TH	F	S
		1	2	3	4	5
6	7	8	9	10	11	12
13	14	15	16	17	18	19
20	21	22	23	24	25	26
27	28	29	30	31		

April 2022						
S	M	T	W	TH	F	S
					1	2
3	4	5	6	7	8	9
10	11	12	13	14	15	16
17	18	19	20	21	22	23
24	25	26	27	28	29	30

2022

MARCH

Sunday 20   First Day of Spring

Monday 21

Tuesday 22

✓

Wednesday 23

Thursday 24

Friday 25

Saturday 26

To-Do List

✓

March 2022

S	M	T	W	TH	F	S
		1	2	3	4	5
6	7	8	9	10	11	12
13	14	15	16	17	18	19
20	21	22	23	24	25	26
27	28	29	30	31		

April 2022

S	M	T	W	TH	F	S
					1	2
3	4	5	6	7	8	9
10	11	12	13	14	15	16
17	18	19	20	21	22	23
24	25	26	27	28	29	30

Shopping List

✓

2022

MAR–APR

Sunday 27

Monday 28

Tuesday 29

Wednesday 30

Thursday 31

Friday 1

Saturday 2

To-Do List

✓

Grief Overturned

I have seen the Lord!   JOHN 20:18

According to Jim and Jamie Dutcher, film-makers known for their knowledge of wolves, when happy, wolves wag their tails and romp about. But after the death of a pack member, they grieve for weeks. They visit the place where the pack member died, showing grief by their drooping tails and mournful howls.

Grief is a powerful emotion we've all experienced, particularly at the death of a loved one or of a treasured hope. Mary Magdalene experienced it. She'd traveled with and helped support Jesus and His disciples (Luke 8:1–3). But His cruel death on a cross separated them. The only thing left for Mary to do for Jesus was to finish anointing His body for burial—a task the Sabbath had interrupted. But imagine how Mary felt when she found not a lifeless, broken body but a living Savior! Though she hadn't at first recognized the man standing before her, when He spoke her name, she knew who He was—Jesus! Instantly, grief turned to joy. Mary now had joyful news to share: "I have seen the Lord!" (John 20:18).

Jesus entered our dark world to bring freedom and life. His resurrection celebrates that He accomplished what He set out to do. We too can celebrate His resurrection and share the good news: He's alive!   LINDA WASHINGTON

2022

APRIL

Sunday	Monday	Tuesday	Wednesday
3	4	5	6
10 Palm Sunday	11	12	13
17 Easter Sunday	18 Easter Monday (Canada)	19	20
24	25	26	27

Praise be to the God and Father of our Lord Jesus Christ! In his great mercy he has given us new birth into a living hope through the resurrection of Jesus Christ from the dead.   —1 PETER 1:3

Thursday	Friday	Saturday	Notes
	1	2	
7	8	9	
14	15	16	
Maundy Thursday	Good Friday	Passover Begins	
21	22	23	
	Earth Day	Passover Ends	
28	29	30	

Shopping List

April 2022

S	M	T	W	TH	F	S
					1	2
3	4	5	6	7	8	9
10	11	12	13	14	15	16
17	18	19	20	21	22	23
24	25	26	27	28	29	30

May 2022

S	M	T	W	TH	F	S
1	2	3	4	5	6	7
8	9	10	11	12	13	14
15	16	17	18	19	20	21
22	23	24	25	26	27	28
29	30	31				

2022

APRIL

Sunday 3

Monday 4

Tuesday 5

Wednesday 6

Thursday 7

Friday 8

Saturday 9

To-Do List

✓

Shopping List

April 2022

S	M	T	W	TH	F	S
					1	2
3	4	5	6	7	8	9
10	11	12	13	14	15	16
17	18	19	20	21	22	23
24	25	26	27	28	29	30

May 2022

S	M	T	W	TH	F	S
1	2	3	4	5	6	7
8	9	10	11	12	13	14
15	16	17	18	19	20	21
22	23	24	25	26	27	28
29	30	31				

2022

APRIL

Sunday 10 Palm Sunday

Monday 11

Tuesday 12

Wednesday 13

Thursday 14 Maundy Thursday

Friday 15 Good Friday

Saturday 16 Passover Begins

To-Do List

✓

Shopping List

April 2022

S	M	T	W	TH	F	S
					1	2
3	4	5	6	7	8	9
10	11	12	13	14	15	16
17	18	19	20	21	22	23
24	25	26	27	28	29	30

May 2022

S	M	T	W	TH	F	S
1	2	3	4	5	6	7
8	9	10	11	12	13	14
15	16	17	18	19	20	21
22	23	24	25	26	27	28
29	30	31				

2022

APRIL

Sunday 17 Easter Sunday

Monday 18 Easter Monday (Canada)

Tuesday 19

Wednesday 20

Thursday 21

Friday 22 Earth Day

Saturday 23 Passover Ends

To-Do List

✓

Shopping List

April 2022

S	M	T	W	TH	F	S
					1	2
3	4	5	6	7	8	9
10	11	12	13	14	15	16
17	18	19	20	21	22	23
24	25	26	27	28	29	30

May 2022

S	M	T	W	TH	F	S
1	2	3	4	5	6	7
8	9	10	11	12	13	14
15	16	17	18	19	20	21
22	23	24	25	26	27	28
29	30	31				

2022

APRIL

Sunday 24

Monday 25

Tuesday 26

Wednesday 27

Thursday 28

Friday 29

Saturday 30

To-Do List

✓

The Saddest Goose

A cord of three strands is not quickly broken.
ECCLESIASTES 4:12

Why is there a football in the parking lot? As I got closer, I realized the greyish lump wasn't a football: it was a goose—the saddest Canada goose I'd ever seen. Geese often congregate on the lawn near my workplace. But today there was only one, its neck arced back and its head tucked beneath a wing. Poor thing was all alone. It looked so lonely, I wanted to give it a hug. (Note: don't try this.)

I've rarely seen a goose completely alone like my lonesome feathered friend. Geese are notably communal, flying in a V-formation to deflect the wind. They're made to be together.

As human beings, we were created for community too (see Genesis 2:18). And in Ecclesiastes 4:10, Solomon describes how vulnerable we are when we're alone: "Woe to him who is alone when he falls, for he has no one to help him up" (NKJV). There's strength in numbers, he added, for "though one may be overpowered, two can defend themselves. A cord of three strands is not quickly broken" (v. 12).

This is just as true for us spiritually as it is physically. God never intended for us to "fly" alone, vulnerably isolated. We need relationships with each other for encouragement, refreshment, and growth (see also 1 Corinthians 12:21). During the extraordinary days of the COVID-19 pandemic, we had to practice physical distancing to help contain the disease. But how we looked forward to the time we could meet face-to-face with our local church families again!

Together, we can stand firm when life's headwinds gust our way. Together. ADAM R. HOLZ

Photo: Poppies of Patmos, Greece; © Alex Soh

MAY

Sunday	Monday	Tuesday	Wednesday
1	2	3	4
8 Mother's Day	9	10	11
15	16	17	18
22	23 Victoria Day (Canada)	24	25
29	30 Memorial Day	31	

The LORD is my strength and my defense; he has become my salvation. He is my God, and I will praise him, my father's God, and I will exalt him. —EXODUS 15:2

Thursday	Friday	Saturday	Notes
5 National Day of Prayer	6	7	
12	13	14	
19	20	21	
26 Ascension Day	27	28	

May 2022

S	M	T	W	TH	F	S
1	2	3	4	5	6	7
8	9	10	11	12	13	14
15	16	17	18	19	20	21
22	23	24	25	26	27	28
29	30	31				

June 2022

S	M	T	W	TH	F	S
			1	2	3	4
5	6	7	8	9	10	11
12	13	14	15	16	17	18
19	20	21	22	23	24	25
26	27	28	29	30		

Shopping List

✓

2022

MAY

Sunday 1

Monday 2

Tuesday 3

Wednesday 4

Thursday 5 National Day of Prayer

Friday 6

Saturday 7

To-Do List

✓

Shopping List

May 2022

S	M	T	W	TH	F	S
1	2	3	4	5	6	7
8	9	10	11	12	13	14
15	16	17	18	19	20	21
22	23	24	25	26	27	28
29	30	31				

June 2022

S	M	T	W	TH	F	S
			1	2	3	4
5	6	7	8	9	10	11
12	13	14	15	16	17	18
19	20	21	22	23	24	25
26	27	28	29	30		

2022

MAY

Sunday 8 Mother's Day

Monday 9

Tuesday 10

Wednesday 11

Thursday 12

Friday 13

Saturday 14

To-Do List

✓

Shopping List

May 2022

S	M	T	W	TH	F	S
1	2	3	4	5	6	7
8	9	10	11	12	13	14
15	16	17	18	19	20	21
22	23	24	25	26	27	28
29	30	31				

June 2022

S	M	T	W	TH	F	S
			1	2	3	4
5	6	7	8	9	10	11
12	13	14	15	16	17	18
19	20	21	22	23	24	25
26	27	28	29	30		

2022

MAY

Sunday 15

Monday 16

Tuesday 17

Wednesday 18

Thursday 19

Friday 20

Saturday 21

To-Do List

✓

Shopping List

✓	....
	....
	....
	....
	....
	....
	....
	....
	....
	....
	....
	....
	....
	....
	....
	....
	....
	....
	....
	....

May 2022

S	M	T	W	TH	F	S
1	2	3	4	5	6	7
8	9	10	11	12	13	14
15	16	17	18	19	20	21
22	23	24	25	26	27	28
29	30	31				

June 2022

S	M	T	W	TH	F	S
			1	2	3	4
5	6	7	8	9	10	11
12	13	14	15	16	17	18
19	20	21	22	23	24	25
26	27	28	29	30		

2022

MAY

Sunday 22

Monday 23 Victoria Day (Canada)

Tuesday 24

Wednesday 25

Thursday 26 Ascension Day

Friday 27

Saturday 28

To-Do List

✓

Promise-Keeper

After waiting patiently, Abraham received what was promised. HEBREWS 6:15

Gripped by the gravity of the promises he was making to LaShonne, Jonathan found himself stumbling as he repeated his wedding vows. He thought, *How can I make these promises and not believe they're possible to keep?* He made it through the ceremony, but the weight of his commitments remained. After the reception, Jonathan led his wife to the chapel where he prayed—for more than two hours—that God would help him keep his promise to love and care for LaShonne.

Jonathan's wedding-day fears were based on the recognition of his human frailties. But God, who promised to bless the nations through Abraham's offspring (Galatians 3:16), has no such limitations. To challenge his Jewish Christian audience to perseverance and patience to continue in their faith in Jesus, the writer of Hebrews recalled God's promises to Abraham, the patriarch's patient waiting, and the fulfillment of what had been promised (Hebrews 6:13–15). Abraham's and Sarah's status as senior citizens was no barrier to the fulfillment of God's promise to give Abraham "many descendants" (v. 14).

Are you challenged to trust God despite being weak, frail, and human? Are you struggling to keep your commitments, to fulfill your pledges and vows? In 2 Corinthians 12:9, God promises to help us: "My grace is sufficient for you, for my power is made perfect in weakness." For more than thirty-six years, God has helped Jonathan and LaShonne to remain committed to their vows. Why not trust Him to help you? ARTHUR JACKSON

Photo: Emerald Lake, British Columbia, Canada; Terry Bidgood © Our Daily Bread Ministries

2022

JUNE

Sunday	Monday	Tuesday	Wednesday
			1
5 Shavuot Pentecost	6	7	8
12	13	14 Flag Day (US)	15
19 Father's Day	20	21 First Day of Summer	22
26	27	28	29

Do not conform to the pattern of this world, but be transformed by the renewing of your mind. Then you will be able to test and approve what God's will is—his good, pleasing and perfect will. —ROMANS 12:2

Thursday	Friday	Saturday	Notes
2	3	4	
9	10	11	
16	17	18	
23	24 St. Jean Baptiste Day (Canada)	25	
30			

Shopping List

June 2022

S	M	T	W	TH	F	S
			1	2	3	4
5	6	7	8	9	10	11
12	13	14	15	16	17	18
19	20	21	22	23	24	25
26	27	28	29	30		

July 2022

S	M	T	W	TH	F	S
					1	2
3	4	5	6	7	8	9
10	11	12	13	14	15	16
17	18	19	20	21	22	23
24	25	26	27	28	29	30
31						

2022

MAY–JUNE

Sunday 29

Monday 30 Memorial Day

Tuesday 31

Wednesday 1

Thursday 2

Friday 3

Saturday 4

To-Do List

✓

Shopping List

June 2022

S	M	T	W	TH	F	S
			1	2	3	4
5	6	7	8	9	10	11
12	13	14	15	16	17	18
19	20	21	22	23	24	25
26	27	28	29	30		

July 2022

S	M	T	W	TH	F	S
					1	2
3	4	5	6	7	8	9
10	11	12	13	14	15	16
17	18	19	20	21	22	23
24	25	26	27	28	29	30
31						

2022

JUNE

Sunday 5   Shavuot
Pentecost

Monday 6

Tuesday 7

Wednesday 8

Thursday 9

Friday 10

Saturday 11

To-Do List

✓

Shopping List

2022

JUNE

Sunday 12

Monday 13

Tuesday 14 Flag Day (US)

Wednesday 15

Thursday 16

Friday 17

Saturday 18

To-Do List

✓

Shopping List

June 2022						
S	M	T	W	TH	F	S
			1	2	3	4
5	6	7	8	9	10	11
12	13	14	15	16	17	18
19	20	21	22	23	24	25
26	27	28	29	30		

July 2022						
S	M	T	W	TH	F	S
					1	2
3	4	5	6	7	8	9
10	11	12	13	14	15	16
17	18	19	20	21	22	23
24	25	26	27	28	29	30
31						

2022

JUNE

Sunday 19 Father's Day

Monday 20

Tuesday 21 First Day of Summer

Wednesday 22

Thursday 23

Friday 24 St. Jean Baptiste Day
(Canada)

Saturday 25

To-Do List

✓

Shopping List

	June 2022						
	S	M	T	W	TH	F	S
				1	2	3	4
	5	6	7	8	9	10	11
	12	13	14	15	16	17	18
	19	20	21	22	23	24	25
	26	27	28	29	30		

	July 2022						
	S	M	T	W	TH	F	S
						1	2
	3	4	5	6	7	8	9
	10	11	12	13	14	15	16
	17	18	19	20	21	22	23
	24	25	26	27	28	29	30
	31						

2022

JUN–JUL

Sunday 26

Monday 27

Tuesday 28

Wednesday 29

Thursday 30

Friday 1 Canada Day

Saturday 2

To-Do List

✓	

Hungry for God

When your words came, I ate them; they were my joy and my heart's delight.

JEREMIAH 15:16

A new believer in Jesus was desperate to read the Bible. However, he'd lost his eyesight and both hands in an explosion. When he heard about a woman who read Braille with her lips, he tried to do the same—only to discover that the nerve endings of his lips had also been destroyed. Later, he was filled with joy when he discovered that he could feel the Braille characters with his tongue! He had found a way to read and enjoy the Scriptures.

The prophet Jeremiah experienced joy and delight when he received God's words. "When your words came, I ate them," he said, "they were my joy and my heart's delight" (Jeremiah 15:16). Unlike the people of Judah who despised His words (8:9), Jeremiah had been obedient and rejoiced in them. His obedience, however, also led to the prophet being rejected by his own people and persecuted unfairly (15:17).

Some of us may have experienced something similar. We once read the Bible with joy, but obedience to God led to suffering and rejection from others. Like Jeremiah, we can bring our confusion to God. He answered Jeremiah by repeating the promise He gave him when He first called him to be a prophet (vv. 19–21; see 1:18–19). God reminded him that He never lets His people down. We can have this same confidence too. He's faithful and will never abandon us. POH FANG CHIA

Photo: Iceland © Will Oechsler

2022

JULY

Sunday	Monday	Tuesday	Wednesday
3	4 Independence Day	5	6
10	11	12	13
17	18	19	20
24 / 31	25	26	27

Surely God is my salvation; I will trust and not be afraid.
*The L*ord*, the L*ord *himself, is my strength and my*
defense; he has become my salvation. —ISAIAH 12:2

Thursday	Friday	Saturday	Notes
	1	2	
	Canada Day		
7	8	9	
14	15	16	
21	22	23	
28	29	30	

Shopping List

✓

2022
JULY

Sunday 3

Monday 4 Independence Day

Tuesday 5

Wednesday 6

Thursday 7

Friday 8

Saturday 9

To-Do List

✓

Shopping List

July 2022

S	M	T	W	TH	F	S
					1	2
3	4	5	6	7	8	9
10	11	12	13	14	15	16
17	18	19	20	21	22	23
24	25	26	27	28	29	30
31						

August 2022

S	M	T	W	TH	F	S
	1	2	3	4	5	6
7	8	9	10	11	12	13
14	15	16	17	18	19	20
21	22	23	24	25	26	27
28	29	30	31			

2022

JULY

Sunday 10

Monday 11

Tuesday 12

Wednesday 13

Thursday 14

Friday 15

Saturday 16

To-Do List

✓

Shopping List

July 2022

S	M	T	W	TH	F	S
					1	2
3	4	5	6	7	8	9
10	11	12	13	14	15	16
17	18	19	20	21	22	23
24	25	26	27	28	29	30
31						

August 2022

S	M	T	W	TH	F	S
	1	2	3	4	5	6
7	8	9	10	11	12	13
14	15	16	17	18	19	20
21	22	23	24	25	26	27
28	29	30	31			

2022

JULY

Sunday 17

Monday 18

Tuesday 19

Wednesday 20

Thursday 21

Friday 22

Saturday 23

To-Do List

✓

July 2022

S	M	T	W	TH	F	S
					1	2
3	4	5	6	7	8	9
10	11	12	13	14	15	16
17	18	19	20	21	22	23
24	25	26	27	28	29	30
31						

August 2022

S	M	T	W	TH	F	S
	1	2	3	4	5	6
7	8	9	10	11	12	13
14	15	16	17	18	19	20
21	22	23	24	25	26	27
28	29	30	31			

Shopping List

✓

2022

JULY

Sunday 24

Monday 25

Tuesday 26

Wednesday 27

Thursday 28

Friday 29

Saturday 30

To-Do List

✓

Run toward Challenge

He looked and saw the hills full of horses and chariots of fire all around Elisha.

2 KINGS 6:17

Tom chased the young men who were stealing his poor friend's bike. He didn't have a plan. He only knew he needed to get it back. To his surprise, the three thieves looked his way, dropped the bike and backed away. Tom was both relieved and impressed with himself as he picked up the bike and turned around. That's when he saw Jeff, his muscular friend who had been trailing close behind.

Elisha's servant panicked when he saw his town surrounded by an enemy army. He ran to Elisha, "Oh no, my lord! What shall we do?" Elisha told him to relax. "Those who are with us are more than those who are with them." Then God opened the servant's eyes, and he "saw the hills full of horses and chariots of fire all around Elisha" (vv. 15–17).

You may also find yourself in some dicey situations. You may have to risk your reputation, and perhaps even your security, because you're determined to do what's right. You may lose sleep wondering how it will all turn out. Remember, you're not alone. You don't have to be stronger or smarter than the challenge before you. Jesus is with you, and His power is greater than all rivals. May we pray for them and others who are running toward the challenges of our day. Ask yourself Paul's question, "If God is for us, who can be against us?" (Romans 8:31). Really, *who*? No one. Run toward your challenge, with God. MIKE WITTMER

AUGUST

Sunday	Monday	Tuesday	Wednesday
	1	2	3
7	8	9	10
14	15	16	17
21	22	23	24
28	29	30	31

You are worthy, our Lord and God, to receive glory and honor and power, for you created all things, and by your will they were created and have their being. —REVELATION 4:11

Thursday	Friday	Saturday	Notes
4	5	6	
11	12	13	
18	19	20	
25	26	27	

August 2022

S	M	T	W	TH	F	S
	1	2	3	4	5	6
7	8	9	10	11	12	13
14	15	16	17	18	19	20
21	22	23	24	25	26	27
28	29	30	31			

September 2022

S	M	T	W	TH	F	S
				1	2	3
4	5	6	7	8	9	10
11	12	13	14	15	16	17
18	19	20	21	22	23	24
25	26	27	28	29	30	

Shopping List

✓

2022

JUL–AUG

Sunday 31

Monday 1

Tuesday 2

Wednesday 3

Thursday 4

Friday 5

Saturday 6

To-Do List

✓

Shopping List

	August 2022							September 2022					
S	M	T	W	TH	F	S	S	M	T	W	TH	F	S
	1	2	3	4	5	6					1	2	3
7	8	9	10	11	12	13	4	5	6	7	8	9	10
14	15	16	17	18	19	20	11	12	13	14	15	16	17
21	22	23	24	25	26	27	18	19	20	21	22	23	24
28	29	30	31				25	26	27	28	29	30	

2022
AUGUST

Sunday 7

Monday 8

Tuesday 9

Wednesday 10

Thursday 11

Friday 12

Saturday 13

To-Do List

✓

Shopping List

August 2022						
S	M	T	W	TH	F	S
	1	2	3	4	5	6
7	8	9	10	11	12	13
14	15	16	17	18	19	20
21	22	23	24	25	26	27
28	29	30	31			

September 2022						
S	M	T	W	TH	F	S
				1	2	3
4	5	6	7	8	9	10
11	12	13	14	15	16	17
18	19	20	21	22	23	24
25	26	27	28	29	30	

2022

AUGUST

Sunday 14

Monday 15

Tuesday 16

Wednesday 17

Thursday 18

Friday 19

Saturday 20

To-Do List

✓

Shopping List

	August 2022								September 2022					
S	**M**	**T**	**W**	**TH**	**F**	**S**		**S**	**M**	**T**	**W**	**TH**	**F**	**S**
	1	2	3	4	5	6						1	2	3
7	8	9	10	11	12	13		4	5	6	7	8	9	10
14	15	16	17	18	19	20		11	12	13	14	15	16	17
21	22	23	24	25	26	27		18	19	20	21	22	23	24
28	29	30	31					25	26	27	28	29	30	

2022
AUGUST

Sunday 21

Monday 22

Tuesday 23

Wednesday 24

Thursday 25

Friday 26

Saturday 27

To-Do List

✓

August 2022

S	M	T	W	TH	F	S
	1	2	3	4	5	6
7	8	9	10	11	12	13
14	15	16	17	18	19	20
21	22	23	24	25	26	27
28	29	30	31			

September 2022

S	M	T	W	TH	F	S
				1	2	3
4	5	6	7	8	9	10
11	12	13	14	15	16	17
18	19	20	21	22	23	24
25	26	27	28	29	30	

Shopping List

✓

2022
AUG–SEP

Sunday 28

Monday 29

Tuesday 30

Wednesday 31

Thursday 1

Friday 2

Saturday 3

To-Do List

✓

A Joyful Celebration

The wedding of the Lamb has come.

REVELATION 19:7

My friend Sharon passed away one year prior to the death of my friend Dave's teenage daughter Melissa. They both had been tragically killed in car accidents. One night both Sharon and Melissa were in my dream. They giggled and talked as they hung streamers in a large banquet hall and ignored me when I stepped into the room. A long table with white tablecloths had been set with golden plates and goblets. I asked if I could help decorate, but they didn't seem to hear me and kept working.

But then Sharon said, "This party is Melissa's wedding reception."

"Who's the groom?" I asked.

Neither responded but smiled and looked at each other knowingly. Finally, it dawned on me—it's Jesus!

"Jesus is the groom," I whispered as I woke up.

My dream brings to mind the joyful celebration believers in Jesus will share together when He returns. It's portrayed in Revelation as a lavish feast called "the wedding supper of the Lamb" (19:9). John the Baptist, who prepared people for the first coming of Christ, had called Him "the Lamb of God, who takes away the sin of the world" (John 1:29). He also referred to Jesus as "the bridegroom" and to himself as the "friend" (like the best man) who waited for Him (3:29).

On that banquet day and for all eternity we will enjoy unbroken fellowship with Jesus, our groom, and with Sharon and Melissa and all of God's people. ANNE CETAS

Photo: Cannonsburg, Michigan, USA;
© Terry Bidgood

2022
SEPTEMBER

Sunday	Monday	Tuesday	Wednesday
4	5 Labor Day Labour Day (Canada)	6	7
11 Grandparents Day	12	13	14
18	19	20	21
25	26 Rosh Hashanah	27	28

Praise be to his glorious name forever; may
the whole earth be filled with his glory.
Amen and Amen. —PSALM 72:19

Thursday	Friday	Saturday	Notes
1	2	3	
8	9	10	
15	16	17	
22 First Day of Autumn	23	24	
29	30		

Shopping List

September 2022							October 2022						
S	M	T	W	TH	F	S	S	M	T	W	TH	F	S
				1	2	3							1
4	5	6	7	8	9	10	2	3	4	5	6	7	8
11	12	13	14	15	16	17	9	10	11	12	13	14	15
18	19	20	21	22	23	24	16	17	18	19	20	21	22
25	26	27	28	29	30		23	24	25	26	27	28	29
							30	31					

2022
SEPTEMBER

Sunday 4

Monday 5   Labor Day
Labour Day (Canada)

Tuesday 6

Wednesday 7

Thursday 8

Friday 9

Saturday 10

To-Do List

✓

Shopping List

September 2022

S	M	T	W	TH	F	S
				1	2	3
4	5	6	7	8	9	10
11	12	13	14	15	16	17
18	19	20	21	22	23	24
25	26	27	28	29	30	

October 2022

S	M	T	W	TH	F	S
						1
2	3	4	5	6	7	8
9	10	11	12	13	14	15
16	17	18	19	20	21	22
23	24	25	26	27	28	29
30	31					

2022
SEPTEMBER

Sunday 11 Grandparents Day

Monday 12

Tuesday 13

Wednesday 14

Thursday 15

Friday 16

Saturday 17

To-Do List

✓

September 2022

S	M	T	W	TH	F	S
				1	2	3
4	5	6	7	8	9	10
11	12	13	14	15	16	17
18	19	20	21	22	23	24
25	26	27	28	29	30	

October 2022

S	M	T	W	TH	F	S
						1
2	3	4	5	6	7	8
9	10	11	12	13	14	15
16	17	18	19	20	21	22
23	24	25	26	27	28	29
30	31					

Shopping List

✓

2022

SEPTEMBER

Sunday 18

Monday 19

Tuesday 20

Wednesday 21

Thursday 22 First Day of Autumn

Friday 23

Saturday 24

To-Do List

✓

September 2022

S	M	T	W	TH	F	S
					1	2	3
4	5	6	7	8	9	10
11	12	13	14	15	16	17
18	19	20	21	22	23	24
25	26	27	28	29	30	

October 2022

S	M	T	W	TH	F	S
						1
2	3	4	5	6	7	8
9	10	11	12	13	14	15
16	17	18	19	20	21	22
23	24	25	26	27	28	29
30	31					

Shopping List

✓

2022

SEP-OCT

Sunday 25

Monday 26 Rosh Hashanah

Tuesday 27

Wednesday 28

Thursday 29

Friday 30

Saturday 1

To-Do List

✓

Hold Steady

I am the LORD your God who takes hold of your right hand.   ISAIAH 41:13

Harriet Tubman was one of the great American heroes of the nineteenth century. Showing remarkable courage, she guided more than three hundred fellow slaves to freedom after she first escaped slavery by crossing into free territory in the United States North. Not content to simply enjoy her own freedom, she ventured back into slave states nineteen times to lead friends, family, and strangers to freedom, sometimes guiding people on foot all the way to Canada.

What drove Tubman to such brave action? A woman of deep faith, she at one time said this: "I always told God, I'm going to hold steady on you, and you've got to see me through." Her dependence on God's guidance as she led people out of slavery was a hallmark of her success.

What does it mean to "hold steady" to God? A verse in the prophecy of Isaiah might help us see that in reality it's He who holds us as we grab His hand. Isaiah quotes God, who said, "I am the LORD your God who takes hold of your right hand and says to you, Do not fear; I will help you" (41:13).

Harriet held tightly to God, and He saw her through. What challenges are you facing? Hold steady to God as He "takes hold" of your hand and your life. "Do not fear." He will help you.   DAVE BRANON

2022

OCTOBER

Sunday	Monday	Tuesday	Wednesday
2	3	4	5 Yom Kippur
9	10 Sukkot Begins Indigenous Peoples' Day/ Columbus Day Thanksgiving Day (Canada)	11	12
16	17	18	19
Sukkot Ends 23	24	25	26
30	31		

You are a chosen people, a royal priesthood, a holy nation, God's special possession, that you may declare the praises of him who called you out of darkness into his wonderful light. —1 PETER 2:9

Thursday	Friday	Saturday	Notes
		1	
6	7	8	
13	14	15	
20	21	22	
27	28	29	

Shopping List

October 2022

S	M	T	W	TH	F	S
						1
2	3	4	5	6	7	8
9	10	11	12	13	14	15
16	17	18	19	20	21	22
23	24	25	26	27	28	29
30	31					

November 2022

S	M	T	W	TH	F	S
		1	2	3	4	5
6	7	8	9	10	11	12
13	14	15	16	17	18	19
20	21	22	23	24	25	26
27	28	29	30			

2022

OCTOBER

Sunday 2

Monday 3

Tuesday 4

Wednesday 5 Yom Kippur

Thursday 6

Friday 7

Saturday 8

To-Do List

✓

Shopping List

✓	

October 2022

S	M	T	W	TH	F	S
						1
2	3	4	5	6	7	8
9	10	11	12	13	14	15
16	17	18	19	20	21	22
23	24	25	26	27	28	29
30	31					

November 2022

S	M	T	W	TH	F	S
		1	2	3	4	5
6	7	8	9	10	11	12
13	14	15	16	17	18	19
20	21	22	23	24	25	26
27	28	29	30			

2022

OCTOBER

Sunday 9

Monday 10 Sukkot Begins
Indigenous Peoples' Day/Columbus Day
Thanksgiving Day (Canada)

Tuesday 11

Wednesday 12

Thursday 13

Friday 14

Saturday 15

To-Do List

✓

Shopping List

October 2022

S	M	T	W	TH	F	S
						1
2	3	4	5	6	7	8
9	10	11	12	13	14	15
16	17	18	19	20	21	22
23	24	25	26	27	28	29
30	31					

November 2022

S	M	T	W	TH	F	S
		1	2	3	4	5
6	7	8	9	10	11	12
13	14	15	16	17	18	19
20	21	22	23	24	25	26
27	28	29	30			

2022

OCTOBER

Sunday 16 Sukkot Ends

Monday 17

Tuesday 18

Wednesday 19

Thursday 20

Friday 21

Saturday 22

To-Do List

✓

Shopping List

October 2022

S	M	T	W	TH	F	S
						1
2	3	4	5	6	7	8
9	10	11	12	13	14	15
16	17	18	19	20	21	22
23	24	25	26	27	28	29
30	31					

November 2022

S	M	T	W	TH	F	S
		1	2	3	4	5
6	7	8	9	10	11	12
13	14	15	16	17	18	19
20	21	22	23	24	25	26
27	28	29	30			

2022

OCTOBER

Sunday 23

Monday 24

Tuesday 25

Wednesday 26

Thursday 27

Friday 28

Saturday 29

To-Do List

✓

Turn on the Light

Let your light shine before others, that they may see your good deeds and glorify your Father in heaven. MATTHEW 5:16

As my husband and I prepared for a cross-country move, I wanted to ensure that we kept in touch with our grown sons. I found a unique gift, friendship lamps connected by wireless internet, which can be turned on remotely. When I gave the lamps to my sons, I explained that their lamps will turn on when I touch my lamp—to provide a shining reminder of my love and ongoing prayers. No matter how great the distance between us, a tap on their lamps would trigger a light in our home too. Though we knew nothing could replace our more personal moments of connection, we could be encouraged by knowing we're loved and prayed for every time we turned on those lights.

All God's children have the privilege of being light-sharers powered by the Holy Spirit. We're designed to live as radiant beacons of God's everlasting hope and unconditional love. When we're sharing the gospel and serving others in the name of Jesus, we become brilliant spotlights and living testimonies. Every good deed, kind smile, gentle word of encouragement, and heartfelt prayer produces a beaming reminder of God's faithfulness and His unconditional and life-transforming love (Matthew 5:14–16).

Wherever God leads us, and however we serve Him, we can be used by Him to help others shine His light. As God, by His Spirit, provides the true illumination, we can reflect the light and love of His presence. XOCHITL DIXON

2022

NOVEMBER

Sunday	Monday	Tuesday	Wednesday
		1	2
6 Daylight Saving Time Ends	7	8	9
13	14	15	16
20	21	22	23
27 Advent Begins	28	29	30

For I am not ashamed of the gospel, because it is the power of God that brings salvation to everyone who believes: first to the Jew, then to the Gentile. —ROMANS 1:16

Thursday	Friday	Saturday	Notes
3	4	5	
10	11 Veterans Day Remembrance Day (Canada)	12	
17	18	19	
24 Thanksgiving Day	25	26	

Shopping List

November 2022

S	M	T	W	TH	F	S
		1	2	3	4	5
6	7	8	9	10	11	12
13	14	15	16	17	18	19
20	21	22	23	24	25	26
27	28	29	30			

December 2022

S	M	T	W	TH	F	S
				1	2	3
4	5	6	7	8	9	10
11	12	13	14	15	16	17
18	19	20	21	22	23	24
25	26	27	28	29	30	31

2022
OCT–NOV

Sunday 30

Monday 31

Tuesday 1

Wednesday 2

Thursday 3

Friday 4

Saturday 5

To-Do List

Shopping List

November 2022

S	M	T	W	TH	F	S
		1	2	3	4	5
6	7	8	9	10	11	12
13	14	15	16	17	18	19
20	21	22	23	24	25	26
27	28	29	30			

December 2022

S	M	T	W	TH	F	S
				1	2	3
4	5	6	7	8	9	10
11	12	13	14	15	16	17
18	19	20	21	22	23	24
25	26	27	28	29	30	31

2022
NOVEMBER

Sunday 6 Daylight Saving Time Ends

Monday 7

Tuesday 8

Wednesday 9

Thursday 10

Friday 11   Veterans Day
Remembrance Day (Canada)

Saturday 12

To-Do List

✓

Shopping List

November 2022

S	M	T	W	TH	F	S
		1	2	3	4	5
6	7	8	9	10	11	12
13	14	15	16	17	18	19
20	21	22	23	24	25	26
27	28	29	30			

December 2022

S	M	T	W	TH	F	S
				1	2	3
4	5	6	7	8	9	10
11	12	13	14	15	16	17
18	19	20	21	22	23	24
25	26	27	28	29	30	31

2022
NOVEMBER

Sunday 13

Monday 14

Tuesday 15

Wednesday 16

Thursday 17

Friday 18

Saturday 19

To-Do List

✓

November 2022

S	M	T	W	TH	F	S
		1	2	3	4	5
6	7	8	9	10	11	12
13	14	15	16	17	18	19
20	21	22	23	24	25	26
27	28	29	30			

December 2022

S	M	T	W	TH	F	S
				1	2	3
4	5	6	7	8	9	10
11	12	13	14	15	16	17
18	19	20	21	22	23	24
25	26	27	28	29	30	31

Shopping List

✓

2022

NOVEMBER

Sunday 20

Monday 21

Tuesday 22

Wednesday 23

Thursday 24 Thanksgiving Day

Friday 25

Saturday 26

To-Do List

✓

Shopping List

November 2022

S	M	T	W	TH	F	S
		1	2	3	4	5
6	7	8	9	10	11	12
13	14	15	16	17	18	19
20	21	22	23	24	25	26
27	28	29	30			

December 2022

S	M	T	W	TH	F	S
				1	2	3
4	5	6	7	8	9	10
11	12	13	14	15	16	17
18	19	20	21	22	23	24
25	26	27	28	29	30	31

2022
NOV-DEC

Sunday 27 Advent Begins

Monday 28

Tuesday 29

Wednesday 30

Thursday 1

Friday 2

Saturday 3

To-Do List

✓

Growing into Giving

Freely you have received; freely give.

MATTHEW 10:8

" I got you a present!" my two-year-old grandson shouted excitedly as he pressed a box into my hands. "He picked it out all by himself," my wife said with a smile.

I opened the box to find a Christmas ornament of his favorite cartoon character. "Can I see it?" he asked anxiously. Then he played with "my" present for the rest of the evening, and as I watched him, I smiled.

I smiled because I remembered gifts I had given loved ones in the past, like the music album I gave my older brother one Christmas when I was in high school that I really wanted to listen to (and did). And I realized how years later God was still stretching me and teaching me to give more unselfishly.

Giving is something we grow into. Paul wrote, "But since you excel in everything . . . see that you also excel in this grace of giving" (2 Corinthians 8:7). Grace fills our giving as we understand that all we have is from God, and He has shown us that "It is more blessed to give than to receive" (Acts 20:35).

God generously gave us the most unselfish gift of all: His only Son, who would die on a cross for our sins and be raised to life. Any who receive this ultimate gift are rich beyond measure. As our hearts are focused on Him, our hands open in love to others. JAMES BANKS

Photo: Last frost-covered apple on tree, Sparta, Michigan, USA © Terry Bidgood

DECEMBER

Sunday	Monday	Tuesday	Wednesday
4	5	6	7
11	12	13	14
18	19 Hanukkah Begins	20	21 First Day of Winter
25 Christmas Day	26 Hanukkah Ends Boxing Day (Canada)	27	28

For to us a child is born, to us a son is given, and the government will be on his shoulders. And he will be called Wonderful Counselor, Mighty God, Everlasting Father, Prince of Peace. —ISAIAH 9:6

Thursday	Friday	Saturday	Notes
1	2	3	
8	9	10	
15	16	17	
22	23	24 Christmas Eve	
29	30	31 New Year's Eve	

Shopping List

December 2022						
S	M	T	W	TH	F	S
					1	2	3
4	5	6	7	8	9	10
11	12	13	14	15	16	17
18	19	20	21	22	23	24
25	26	27	28	29	30	31

January 2023						
S	M	T	W	TH	F	S
1	2	3	4	5	6	7
8	9	10	11	12	13	14
15	16	17	18	19	20	21
22	23	24	25	26	27	28
29	30	31				

2022
DECEMBER

Sunday 4

Monday 5

Tuesday 6

Wednesday 7

Thursday 8

Friday 9

Saturday 10

To-Do List

✓

Shopping List

December 2022

S	M	T	W	TH	F	S
					1	2	3
4	5	6	7	8	9	10
11	12	13	14	15	16	17
18	19	20	21	22	23	24
25	26	27	28	29	30	31

January 2023

S	M	T	W	TH	F	S
1	2	3	4	5	6	7
8	9	10	11	12	13	14
15	16	17	18	19	20	21
22	23	24	25	26	27	28
29	30	31				

2022

DECEMBER

Sunday 11

Monday 12

Tuesday 13

Wednesday 14

Thursday 15

Friday 16

Saturday 17

To-Do List

✓

Shopping List

December 2022

S	M	T	W	TH	F	S
				1	2	3
4	5	6	7	8	9	10
11	12	13	14	15	16	17
18	19	20	21	22	23	24
25	26	27	28	29	30	31

January 2023

S	M	T	W	TH	F	S
1	2	3	4	5	6	7
8	9	10	11	12	13	14
15	16	17	18	19	20	21
22	23	24	25	26	27	28
29	30	31				

2022
DECEMBER

Sunday 18

Monday 19 Hanukkah Begins

Tuesday 20

Wednesday 21   First Day of Winter

Thursday 22

Friday 23

Saturday 24   Christmas Eve

To-Do List

✓

December 2022

S	M	T	W	TH	F	S
				1	2	3
4	5	6	7	8	9	10
11	12	13	14	15	16	17
18	19	20	21	22	23	24
25	26	27	28	29	30	31

January 2023

S	M	T	W	TH	F	S
1	2	3	4	5	6	7
8	9	10	11	12	13	14
15	16	17	18	19	20	21
22	23	24	25	26	27	28
29	30	31				

Shopping List

✓

2022

DECEMBER

Sunday 25 Christmas Day

Monday 26 Hanukkah Ends
Boxing Day (Canada)

Tuesday 27

Wednesday 28

To-Do List

Thursday 29

Friday 30

Saturday 31 New Year's Eve

IMPORTANT CONTACTS

Name: ....

Address: ....

City: .... State: .... Zip: ....

Mobile Phone: .... Email: ....
....

Name: ....

Address: ....

City: .... State: .... Zip: ....

Mobile Phone: .... Email: ....
....

Name: ....

Address: ....

City: .... State: .... Zip: ....

Mobile Phone: .... Email: ....
....

Name: ....

Address: ....

City: .... State: .... Zip: ....

Mobile Phone: .... Email: ....

IMPORTANT CONTACTS

Name:

Address:

City: State: Zip:

Mobile Phone: Email:

Name:

Address:

City: State: Zip:

Mobile Phone: Email:

Name:

Address:

City: State: Zip:

Mobile Phone: Email:

Name:

Address:

City: State: Zip:

Mobile Phone: Email:

IMPORTANT CONTACTS

Name:

Address:

City: State: Zip:

Mobile Phone: Email:

Name:

Address:

City: State: Zip:

Mobile Phone: Email:

Name:

Address:

City: State: Zip:

Mobile Phone: Email:

Name:

Address:

City: State: Zip:

Mobile Phone: Email:

IMPORTANT CONTACTS

Name:

Address:

City: State: Zip:

Mobile Phone: Email:

Name:

Address:

City: State: Zip:

Mobile Phone: Email:

Name:

Address:

City: State: Zip:

Mobile Phone: Email:

Name:

Address:

City: State: Zip:

Mobile Phone: Email:

IMPORTANT CONTACTS

Name:

Address:

City: State: Zip:

Mobile Phone: Email:

Name:

Address:

City: State: Zip:

Mobile Phone: Email:

Name:

Address:

City: State: Zip:

Mobile Phone: Email:

Name:

Address:

City: State: Zip:

Mobile Phone: Email:

IMPORTANT CONTACTS

Name:

Address:

City: State: Zip:

Mobile Phone: Email:

Name:

Address:

City: State: Zip:

Mobile Phone: Email:

Name:

Address:

City: State: Zip:

Mobile Phone: Email:

Name:

Address:

City: State: Zip:

Mobile Phone: Email:

NOTES

NOTES

NOTES

NOTES

NOTES

NOTES

NOTES

NOTES

HELPING YOU CONNECT WITH GOD EVERY DAY

You can receive your daily devotional by mail, Email, web, app, or e-book. Sign up today!

odb.org/subscribe

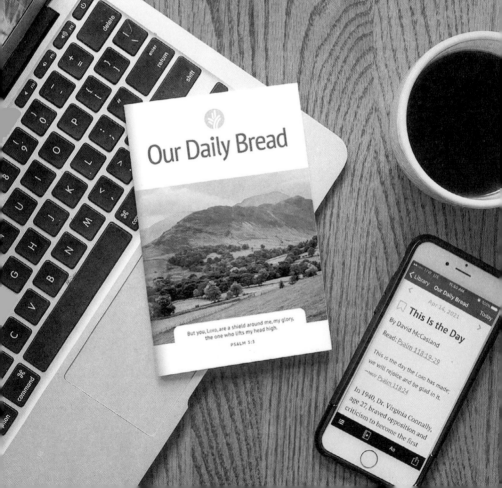